I0422920

Cats For Kids
Amazing Animal Books
For Young Readers

K. Bennett

Mendon Cottage Books

JD-Biz Publishing

Read More Amazing Animal Books

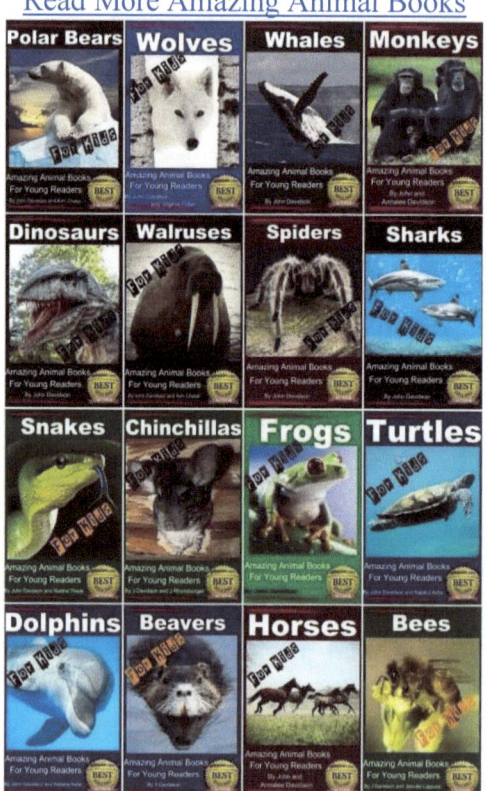

Purchase at Amazon.com

Download Free Books!
http://MendonCottageBooks.com

Table of Contents

Introduction

The smallest feline is a masterpiece.
Leonardo da Vinci

Have you ever thought of a cat as masterpiece in motion? There is no doubt cats are fascinating creatures, from the tip of their ears all the way to their furry little toes!

Cats have a rich history going back many years, long before you and I were even born. Many nations, but especially ancient Egypt, worshiped cats as gods and goddesses. Some Egyptians loved their cats like family, and gave them beautiful jewelry to wear around their necks. However, other nations feared this unique creature and tried to destroy them, only to realize much later how important cats truly are.

Thankfully, cats survived, and today are one of the most popular pets in the United States. But they are not *only* pets. Did you know some cats even ran for office?

In the small town of Talkeetna, Alaska a fun loving cat called Stubbs won the election! And it has been reported that he's an excellent mayor. But that's not all. He even has his own Facebook page affectionately called ***Mayor Stubbs***.

Cats and dogs also have quite an interesting history, even though most people claim the animals hate each other on sight! While that may be true in some cases, in others it is quite the opposite. **The Journal for Applied Animal Behavior Science** published an article in 2008, which explained the problem between cats and dogs. It's something that affects us as people too! Have you guessed yet? Well, it's quite simple. It's called…*"lack of communication."*

Don't be surprised at this fact. Just like us, if cats and dogs don't "talk things out" they won't get along. So the Journal noted the importance of introducing the feline and the canine (Cat and dog), early on in life. In other words, they should be introduced at less than 6 months old. If they are, then both cat and dog will *understand* each other and coexist together in peace!

Kitten & Puppy playing together

Perhaps this plan will not work for every single cat, but it's worth a try. Of course cats have a very unique personality, and some may even be a bit moody. But on the whole, they are a beautiful expression of nature's great diversity!

 **Chapter 1**

There are many kinds of cats including Big Cats (Lion, Tiger, Leopard, Jaguar and more) but for the purpose of this book, we will focus on the domesticated cat and their features.

A cat's life starts out as a beautiful little fur ball called a kitten. The mother's "litter" can have from one to five or even more cats at one time. But usually, it's between two and five kittens per litter. Aren't they precious?

British Kittens

How does a cat's life *begin*?

The gestation period of cats is between 64-67 days. The term "gestation" simply means how long the mother cat carries the little baby kittens inside her tummy.

When the kittens are born, they come out in a little sac called an *amnion*. This sac protects the baby kitten inside the mother's tummy and once the kitten is born, the sac is no longer needed.

The mother cat takes the sac away from the baby, and lovingly "bathes" the little kitten with her tongue, so its fur can get clean and fluffy.

For the first three weeks the kitten is very dependent on the mother to keep the right temperature in its little body. If the mother doesn't keep it warm, the baby will get too cold and its life could be in danger.

What do kittens *eat* and why?

During the first days of a kitten's life, the right food is very important to its development. *But not just any kind of food*. The kitten needs specific milk (and only milk) from its mother that will help it to stay healthy. This milk has special antibodies that will help the kitten to fight off dangerous infections.

Of course eating is not the only thing the baby cat loves to do. During these first few days, the baby kitten still has its eyes closed. So it depends on the nearness of its mother to know everything is all right. Since there is usually more than one kitten, all enjoy the benefit from being close to each other. This bond will serve them well during the next few weeks.

Early development

Between the ages of 2-7 weeks, kittens start to develop at a rapid rate. They get much stronger. Their coordination improves, and their curiosity explodes!

Once they start to wander around the nest, they become intrepid explorers! No corner is too dark, and no obstacle too large to avoid some inspection.

But exploring is not the only thing they do. The kittens play with their baby brothers and sisters, but they also fight with them. This fighting is not a real fight. The kittens are not upset. They are simply using the skills they will need later on in life. So you can call this action *play-fight* instead.

Hunting games and stalking games are also part of the kitten's life, where they hide behind objects and *pounce* on their "prey". Each skill gets better with time, and helps a baby kitten to become a formidable hunter.

What about the mother cat? She doesn't stand by and leave her kittens all to themselves. She helps them to improve their skills, by bringing *live prey* to the nest. She also demonstrates hunting techniques, and her baby kittens learn a lot from her.

As the kittens get a little bit older, it's time to leave the mother's milk to dine on solid food. This does not mean they will not suckle their mother's milk after their taste of solid food. Sometimes the mother has to shoo them away! But in some cases, the mother will allow them to suckle even when they are almost bigger than her. I had a cat like that, and it was funny to see kittens almost the size of their mother still drinking milk! Gladly for the mother's sake, this does not always happen.

As time goes by, kittens lose their baby teeth and by 9 months they have their adult teeth. Their social life expands, and they play with just about anything or anyone they can find. Eventually this form of play will expand to cover a greater distance where the kitten will wander away to hunt and stalk alone.

Kitten playing alone

Best *time* to get a new cat?

It is customary for new kittens to find a home during the 6th to 8th week of their life. However, there is some concern that this may be too young. Why? Well, remember kittens are developing skills they will need later on. And during the 6th to 12th week, kittens receive valuable training to help their social skills. Behavioral skills are also perfected during this time.

For the most part someone who sells kittens will not part with them under 12 weeks, and in some places it is illegal to give them away under 8 weeks.

I know it's exciting to get a new pet but if you want a baby kitten, try to be patient, and give it the time it needs to be ready. Your baby kitten will thank you for being so kind to think about its needs.

And if you want to get a new kitten, perhaps you could think about adopting one. If your parents agree, let them take you to a Pet center and look over the kittens to find the perfect one… just for you!

 **Chapter 2**

3 Oriental cats & 2 Siamese cats

There are many different species of cats, some with very exotic names and behaviors from around the world. Would you like meet 3 of them?

 **Fascinating Cat Species**

Balinese:

This feline is blessed with a beautiful variation of sapphire blue eyes, which can range from light to a deeper hue, depending on the age and diet. Another name for the Balinese cat is Long-haired Siamese. Because of this, it has soft silky hair and a plumed tail, making it quite an attractive addition to the cat family.

Balinese love to talk, and to keep on talking. So they may not appeal to everyone especially if you want to sleep, and your cat only wants to talk!

But they are very sensitive to their surroundings, and they are ever attentive to your emotions. If you are feeling down and need a little happiness, your Balinese cat will be ready to lift you up until you feel better.

They are very athletic and wouldn't think twice to hop on your shoulders and rest there comfortably. Also quite teachable, they learn to play fetch very easily, and interact very well with their surroundings. Some are even *tech savvy* if such a term can apply to a cat!

Chartreux:

This cat makes a wonderful companion, and they are famous not only for their loyalty, but for their amiable behavior too. They are quite friendly and adaptable. And unlike the Balinese, they keep their "voice" to themselves. In other words, they can be as quiet as a church mouse!

However, just like us, they can get a bit moody from time to time. But they are very smart and have a good sense of humor. Did you know this cat has a comical side? Yes, they do! Sometimes their behavior has been termed "silly" which can be a lot of fun to watch.

Chartruex love to "pounce" on things, tearing toys to pieces if allowed. And they carry it off with perfect acrobatic flips and splendid timing. However, for the most part, the cat is curious about one thing, and that's *you*!

They love to observe your actions to see what you're doing, and remain nearby to keep your company. They are attentive and would love it if you spared a moment to scratch them between the ears, or just below the chin. You don't need to worry that the cat will pester you to death if you don't have the time. For the most part, this cat is content to wander around at your footsteps, and offer loving attention just when you need it!

Where their personality is concerned the Chartreux may not greet your neighbors with love and affection. Usually they are not very sociable, although they can warm up after a while.

Generally speaking, this cat is a *"wait and see what happens"* kind of feline. They like to scope out the land, and if all is well, they may decide to jump into the mix. If not, they will find something else to do, until they have you all to themselves!

Chartreux Cat, 16 months old

Egyptian Mau:

Did you know "Mau" is the Egyptian word for Cat?

The Egyptian Mau is a beautiful feline with a spotted coat. This is a very agile cat, who loves to play fetch. But the Egyptian Mau can be a fierce hunter so if you play games similar to hunting, you can expect the Mau to join in the fun!

A wonderful feature about this cat is the fierce devotion it pays to their owners. Mostly, the Mau doesn't get along with strangers. They are more of a "one cat, one family" kind of feline. But this is a great feature in a cat. You know that once it "bonds" with you, it will not bond with another.

They don't speak that much, but if they have to complain about something, they will, especially when it comes to their food dish! However, their voice is quite musical, so you won't have any complaints about the tone. The Mau's vocal sounds have been described as a chortle or chirp, among other unusual vocalizations.

The Mau also does a curious little happy dance when it's contented. It does a "wiggle-tail" movement you may find enchanting. And if you look closely you may observe the dark markings of the letter M on the Mau's forehead!

Egyptian Mau

Some say the lines on the forehead looks like the mark of a scarab

beetle. What do you think?

Chapter 3 - A Cat's History

Somali Cats

Cats have a rich history dating back thousands of years, if not more. Back in those days, cats did not live with people, and spent their time outdoors sharing their existence with other wildlife.

During the time of the shipping boom, cats were prized as mousers. They were exceptional at catching and getting rid of vermin. In this way, cats traveled around the globe with their masters and soon they spread all over. From Egypt to Rome and the Americas, cats have been a part of people's lives for a long time.

However, not everyone loves cats. Why not? Mostly because of a cat's personality. A cat can be a very independent being. He or she can pretty much take care of themselves if necessary, so in a way, they don't really need us! Don't worry. This doesn't mean that we can't live together as friends. In fact many cats are now the dearest and best friends of many people around the world.

So, what makes a cat so independent? Some say it's because cats remember how they were worshipped many years ago. Did you know in Ancient Egypt cats were seen as gods? I mentioned this in the introduction, but let me expand on the topic just a little.

BAST was the protector of domestic cats. Usually she was represented as a woman with a cat's head or a cat herself. Her protection of cats expanded to daily life. You could get into a lot of trouble if you hurt a cat, even accidentally. And when a cat died, the owners felt so hurt they would shave off their eyebrows to show their distress.

Bast was not the only one with a cat figure. There were others such as **Sekmet**. She had the head of a lion. Then there was **Mau**, thought to be a personification of Ra and **Tefnut**, another goddess with the head of a lioness.

So the Egyptian culture placed cats on a high pedestal. Because of the degree of trade during the Egyptian era, cats traveled to other nations and cultures, which included the Phoenicians, the Celts, the Gaels and the Romans.

Closer to our timeline in 1895, there was a show held in Madison Square Garden. Can you guess what kind of show it was? Yes! A cat show. It was the first of its kind. Officially it was called "The National Cat Show," and a beautiful Maine Coon Cat by the name of Cosey won the award, and received a silver cat collar as a prize!

Of course history is not the only reason a cat may feel independent. There is some discussion as to the difference in genetics between dogs and cats. Whether the reasons are based on this or not, there is no doubt a cat has a measure of independence. But it doesn't mean they don't love to be around you. They only have a different way of showing it!

 **A Cat's Life**

Cats can live for approximately 20 years. And some cats have lived a bit longer than that. The basic reason why is this: Cat years and human years are two different things, and they are calculated differently as well. How? Did you know there is an actual cat calculator? Let's see how it works.

Traci Hotcher wrote a book called *the cat bible*. And in this book she details the following list you may find interesting.

-A 1-month-old kitten is equal to a 6 month old human baby

-A 3-month-old kitten is equal to a 4 year old child

-A 6-month-old kitten is equal to a 10 year old child

-An 8 month old kitten is equal to a 15 year old

-A 1-year-old cat is now an adult, and is equal to an 18 year old

To put it further into perspective consider the following:

-A 2 year old human is equal to 24 cat years

-A 4 year old human is equal to 35 cat years

-A 6 year old human is equal to 42 cat years

-An 8 year old human is equal to 50 cat years

-A 10 year old human is equal to 60 cat years

-A 12 year old human is equal to 70 cat years

-A 14 year old human is equal to 80 cat years

-A 16 year old human is equal to 84 cat years

So as the years go by, your cat is aging much faster than you are! There is an actual cat calculator online where you can check the age of your cat to see exactly how old he or she is. But before you search, ask your parent's or an adult's permission.

Fascinating Features

As we have seen, cats are fascinating creatures and you may know a lot about them, but did you know they still have the ability to surprise us?

Here are some intriguing details you may not know about these amazing felines.

-Have you ever seen a cat drinking milk? The process is not as simple as you might think. First the cat touches the liquid with the tip of its tongue. Once the tongue makes contact with the surface, a column of milk stretches from one end to the other. The interesting thing is despite the effect of gravity and before the milk can slip back down into the dish, the cat snaps its mouth shut trapping the liquid inside.

-Cats can control your actions with a *single* cry. A study done in 2009 reveals how susceptible we are to the specific purr of our felines. Why? It turns out the frequency of the purr is something we can't ignore. The sound is quite similar to the effect of a baby's cry. Have you ever heard a baby crying and felt the need to respond right away? The purr of a cat provokes the same urge to act.

-Cats have formidable kidneys that work much better than our own. Did you know cats can drink sea water to rehydrate if necessary? Can you drink sea water to quench your thirst? Neither can I! But a cat can do it. Isn't that amazing?

-Cat's learn quickly! And you can teach them to use a litter box quite easily. First get your box ready. More than likely your cat will sniff around the object to see what you are doing. It's their way of saying *"Oh wow, something new to explore!"* Then put your kitty in it. They might jump out, but if you repeat the process just a bit more, they will get the hang of it. You could also use their paw to scratch at the surface. Each step will teach your kitty exactly what they need to do, and soon you won't have to teach them at all!

A word to the wise: Some cats are not too easy to teach, so have a little patience, and your efforts will be rewarded.

-Did you know a cat's urine can glow? Yes it can! But you need a special light to see it called backlight or ultraviolet light.

- Cats can survive a fall from a great height. Some have survived even though they fell from 32 stories to the concrete pavement below.

-Cats love to sleep! Approximately 70% of its life is spent snoozing away. That's a lot of sleeping don't you think?

- If you own a cat, you may live longer. Do you know why? It has been said their companionship reduces the risk of stroke and heart attack.

- Cats can make a lot of different sounds. In comparison to dogs cats can make about 100 different sounds, and dogs make around 10.

- When a cat gets really upset you may hear a ferocious hiss or an angry growl. Perhaps at this moment it will be wise to let them calm down just a bit before you pet them!

Cats are truly amazing creatures, but these are not the only fascinating features of cats. There is a lot more we can learn if we simply take the time to see… just how wonderful a cat can be!

Conclusion

Cats are in a league all their own. They can be independent, solitary, moody, mysterious and even aloof. However, they can also be loving, kind, affectionate, funny, composed, regal and fiercely loyal. And like most of us they have good days and bad days!

But on the whole, cats are a unique part of nature's great tapestry of wonders. So if you have a cat or would like to get one, remember their devotion to you…

"Meow, Meowww, Meowwme, Meowwwrrr, Meowesss, Meowwwr, Meowww, Mewoooww, Meeeowwm, Meow, Meowwwr, Meowwme, Meowwwrrr, Meowesss, Meowwwr, Meowwwr"

Do you know that this means?

In the cat tongue it reads: "*Just love me, and I'll love you too. Just hold me, and I'll be forever true.*"

Author Bio

K. Bennett is a native from the Island of Roatan in the Caribbean, North of Honduras. She loves to write about many things, but writing for children is dear to her heart.

Some of her favorite pastimes are reading, traveling and discovering new things, all of which help to fuel her imagination for more stories.

Her writing credits include local newspaper articles, blogs at Helium.com and Wordpress.com. It also includes real estate articles at Condo.com, two children books online, and two novellas listed on Amazon.com

Our books are available at

1. Amazon.com

2. Barnes and Noble

3. Itunes

4. Kobo

5. Smashwords

6. Google Play Books

Download Free Books!
http://MendonCottageBooks.com

Publisher

JD-Biz Corp

P O Box 374

Mendon, Utah 84325

http://www.jd-biz.com/

www.ingramcontent.com/pod-product-compliance
Lightning Source LLC
Chambersburg PA
CBHW050907290526
45792CB00002B/722